Noted

Aishah Bomani

To my family,
that always
believed I
could.
Thank you.

Part I

He said,
It's always been you
As he searched for me everywhere.

Breathing

Feeling emotions has nothing do with
experience
Yet everything to do with
understanding
So don't read to feel
Breathe to understand that
When you let something in
Then something comes out
And whatever that may be
It may not always make a sound
Hence, we become lost
And the only way we are found
Is to let something in
Even when it's not always announced
You must feel an experience
You might not ever understand

How Cliché

Loving you was like a cliche I tried
to make work but fell flat on my ass.
And after I had fallen on my ass your
ass extended your hand to help me back
up.
"Bounce back" were your words
cushioned between an apology and a
gratifying
Smile because it's such a cliche that
a good girl goes for the bad boy
The good girl gets played like a toy
The good girl gave you joy
The good girl you employed
That same girl's trust destroyed
Anyone can say that there's two sides
and I'm just a heartbroken shattered
over exaggerated combative chick that
threatens to throw a tantrum because
you won't listen and look at what you
did
Let go move on push through
All the things I did to even speak to
you
The way my anxiety is set up is like
don't talk at all unless spoken to and
then when you're sure it's you

Ignore until he approaches you
Ignore until he mentions you
Ignore until he...
Waited for months and then
Something like the beginning of our
love story began and you were the
first one to jump in
Making it easy for me to swim around
the idea that we were just cruising
the shallow end
Was so caught up I head scared to
drown in something deep
Kicking and stroking to stay afloat
Too much going on to see you ghost
Me without a goodbye
Without a reason why
I mean couldn't you have been a cliché
and lie?
Tell me how beautiful I was
That I was the only one
Thank me for the time spent making
cliches
Break because it's such a cliche that
a bad boy loses a good girl
The bad boy couldn't learn to wait
The bad body then went and set a date
The bad boy chose culture over fate
The bad boy walked away

Needs

You don't need me
And I more importantly decided I don't
need you
Needs
As frivolous as our desires
As fluctuating as our faith
As feverish as our emotions
But I don't need you either
If we are true mirrors to one another
I reflect your independence
I exude your selfishness
I represent your growth
Moving on from childish daydreams to
grown man plans
A wife to hold in your hands
Speak in your tongue
Even though I was fluent in your
love language
You didn't need me
To be the peace at the end of the day
To be the womb where your seed could
lay
To be the half to complete your faith
We had the moon and stars
You were looking for the sun
We had a vibe the preceded this realm

You were looking for reality
We had all the laughs
You were looking for memories
I didn't need you
To heal me
To take care of me
To save me
You didn't need me
To care
To love
To wait
For you there was no condition
For you there was only submission
I don't need an apology
You don't need to be sorry
I don't need to matter
You don't need to write me off
I don't need to move on
Yet
You need me to and already have
We don't need to need our needs that
lead us back to whatever we created
But the need still burns
To see you
To be with me
To check on you
To call me yours
To pray for us

To forget us
Medicate in the absentness

Appearances

You see me
You laugh with me
Eat with me
Make jokes with me
Make jokes about me
Make jokes about everyone else
You see me
Working hard
Providing for my hand
Striving to please the Most High
Keeping a smile at all times
You see me
Ask how you are
Check in with you again
Make sure you've eaten
Ask about the family
Are you good?
You see me
Zoning out of the conversations
Eyes drift off to a place where I'm
Safe
My heart slows down after a game of
chase
Wishing we really were about that
mirror life
You see me

But you don't wanna see yourself
In me
Through me
With me
So you won't love for me
What you have loved for yourself
Peace
Love
Light

He who does not love for his brother

An Attempt to Woe

I could write a love poem
Drown you in my feelings
Tell you all the things
The songs today are missing
Like can we talk for a minute?
I wanna know
Can you stand the rain?
But you don't like to sing
Maybe you can humble down and serenade
me with vulnerability
Tell me all the things some brothers
don't
That I'm the Queen you'll protect
And that you need love
It could all be so simple
The more you say
The bigger my dimples
And if you would only swing my way
You'd know those dimples don't exist
Maybe this conversation needs to
happen
Off of text
Flip and reverse it
All of this just a rehearsed mix
Of how I want you
Want you?

No
Maybe
Yeah
Want you
Write a love poem want you

Blue Bound

He has a box of crayons
But he'll only draw in Blue
Too naïve to let go of what he won't
use
Too scared to give away what he thinks
he might lose
Too damaged from the past to try
something new
Phased marriages
Faded images
He'd empty the ocean
Seeking what is already sought
Holding on to the Blue crayon
Til death do them part

Neglect

Is it raining or are those drops just
Falling from the roof?
Does the hawk fly or glide through the
sky?
When you breath in what sound does it
make?
When you release who's name do you
speak?
Can you smell flowers with your eyes?
And see color with your nose?
Or taste with your hand and feel with
your mouth?
Will your heart keep beating if you
tell it to stop?
Do you have the power to unsee?
How do you decide a decision that's
been decided?
What language do you hear in and how
many languages does your tongue hold?
Which pleasures have you forsaken your
soul?
Who gave you the power of future, who
blinded you from the present, who are
you putting in your past?
After all is said and done, the answer,
like me,
always comes last.

Take me Home

He said a broken heart
Is a heart that's been opened
Yet I came into this world
With a heart that's never known
wholeness
The light you try to beam
The words you aim to fill it with
The seeds you want to plant
All fall to an empty soul
No tears to water
No womb to cultivate them
No flesh to turn
This body carries a spirt
A spirit waiting to return
To a world unknown
And a realm already tasted
To bring back what is missing inside
me
That which cannot be broke
That which needs no opening
That which is felt and not seen

Empty name

Please don't say my name
When you don't say anything after

You ask for gentleness
I ask for effort

But when I ask how you are
And you don't ask me

It's a gentle reminder that
I'm just another name

Maybe if my heart
Were made of glass
And not stone
Your light could
Shine through

Maybe if your light
Had some warmth
And not just empty words
The heat would
Crack through

Maybe if those cracks
Broke deep enough
And not just on the surface
Your light could

Shine through

Maybe the shine
Can fill the gaps
And help transform
My stone heart
To light

Pulse Check

Dear Heart,
Yes, this could be circumstantial
Or this could be an example
A reflection of him
Your mirror didn't want to reflect
Until now
When the world had stilled itself to
you
And removed the noise and chaos
But you were already use to the
silence
Long before the virus
And the social distance
He's washed his hands
Cleaning me from his existence
Or this could be a test
The way we tell ourselves
Truths we aren't ready to accept

Lost at Sea

The first time
I went to the sea
It sang a song
Called poetry

When it was done
It walked with me
To drink some fruity drinks
In good company

I watched it wait
In agony
Then it asked me
If I had a remedy

My hand offered relief
My heart skipped a beat
You pulled out a chair
And offered me a seat

And suddenly
The waves pushed you away
Only to return
After the weather changed

You remembered me

I greeted you
You asked about me
I answered you

You were always
Washing up on shores
Singing your songs
Missing you more

One time you stayed
Longer than before
Transforming me
Refining my core

As I got comfortable
You were back to sea
Crossing oceans
Forgetting me

And the last time
We spoke
Words were short
I lost hope

So I wrote poetry
Thinking you'd come back
If there was a reason
For the waves to put us back on track

Your ripples teased me
Inviting me in
But not to stay
Just a drop in the ocean

You remained unfazed
Splashing for attention
Everywhere else
Creating tension

I wanted more than you could give
Songs and poetry that gave me life
Was just a notion
To becoming your wife

I didn't realize that the sea
Was no longer looking to explore
The boats it sailed were anchored
And all accounted for

Singing songs
Called poetry
Time after time with
Every visit from the sea

Victim of Self

Who haven't I loved
That hasn't hurt me
I am convinced that being in pain
means
Living
And if you're living
Without any pain
You can't really be living
Love can be blind
And get you thinking
That rose are red
Violets are blue
And if you love back
They won't hurt you
Or the pain goes away
These words might not be your truth
But you can't deny that what I say is
true
And in your love for me
Convince yourself you will be
different
The exception
The one
Making promises to never...
Just stop because the most
Painful wounds are by the tongue

Each word
Strikes a nerve
No Band-Aid or ice to apply
Just raw hurt spewing from the inside
out
Tears fall in familiar rhythms
A reminder that living
Gives you wisdom

Wishful mornings

Each day I open my eye
One by one
And look to the side
That's been unslept
Unclaimed

Some days I reach out
And touch the pillow
Where another head should rest
And breathe in a different
But familiar scent

Most of the time
I just roll over
And cool off
Before I jump out
To start the day

But today
Today I woke up
Breathing your name
And when I rolled over
I felt your embrace

So when I saw your face
Later that day

My face turned red
But I couldn't look away

You went on and on
And I listened
Waiting for a chance
To tell you that
I've already seen our future

Selfie for the Soul

Perception of my mirror image has
fallen short of the sight
Of the self-proclaimed vision
Unshadowed by the Light

Frame me with the best filters
Blur it all together
Measures to reflect the perfect image
All to send and be delivered

I am not what I am in
Nor am I in what you see
And what you see is
A sapling from a divine seed

Listen to hear the leaves
Singing whispers in the sky
A claim I will never make
and an accusation I will never deny.

Free-write

I retire from this pen
Its ink no longer shows up
To be read
And I can no longer spin words for
webs
Meant to trap you
No

I free the pen of writing anything
with force
Pressed with paper imprints
Like muscle memory maybe that's why
all my poems sound the same
Yes

I continue to scribe scripted
perceptive narratives
No pen needed
Just playing out in my head
Thanks to the Moon's spotlight
And clouds move between the seen
No

I wrote poems before knowing what a
poem was
Before they were graded and torn

Before spoken word was a norm
Before poems were passed as
invitations
Before snaps and encores
Yes

Reunion

I love you without knowing
how
or when
or from where...
I love you simply

Simply as inhaling air
From the highest point of the mountain
And exhaling into the deep blue sea
My love, you are the end to my means

Means to love you
Heartbeat to heartbeat
Knees to knees
Dancing hummingbirds
Peonies to honeybees
All of you, simply within me
All of me, simply within you

You pull me to and from
Deep blues of joy
Then you simply dispatch
Gone like a decoy
But my love, you always come back
To revive the light

Light to a line we cry over every time
Simply plunging cold waters
That revive familiar paradigms
To continue to love each other
"In and out
In and out
In and out of time" *

*

*In and Out of Time- Maya Angelou

Love[3]

Puddles of tears behind the eyes
kissed away
by memories

Morning breath smiles
Laughter all day
Goodnight kisses

new lips
new fingertips
new imprints

Memories being made
Trusting the familiar
Hoping for a new fate

old habits
old songs
old pictures

Inhaling the moment
Holding it present
Exhaling the fear

To live in this world
You must be able
to do three things:

Love
Love Again
And love again.

Oath of Silence

My pen took an oath of silence
10 years
Of words unwritten
Words forgotten
Memories untraced
Memories left to fade

My pen took an oath of silence
10 years
Carrying guilt
Carrying the words unspoken
No tears
No help

My pen took an oath of silence
10 years
Of forgetting my dreams
Forgetting to dream
Remembering your dreams
Remembering to continue your legacy

My pen took an oath of silence
10 years
New grandchildren
New marriages
Old habits

Old secrets

My pen took an oath of silence
10 years
Of denial
Pretending
Laughing
Trying

My pen took an oath of silence
10 years
To finally break
Finally speak
Finding the magic word
Accepting grief

Walking Nightmare

I drove on a dark cloud in the middle
of December
Pulled up and somehow landed at your
door
Or was it a different number?
See I couldn't really remember and
even now when I recall all I can tell
you was that it was a night in
December
You would say I called but a phone I
can't trace and the numbers blocked so
pulling up was the only way
In bed I lay and talked to God and
tried to pray because everything was
about to go wrong
And before I could even let it all
play out so that I give my brain a
reason to wrestle with doubt
I knocked and you wouldn't come out
Knock knock
All the doors were white or maybe they
brown
Maybe we went the other way and I need
to turnaround
Mirror Mirror on the wall

Why wouldn't you take my call?
Or maybe you did
I remembered a Mirror and that's where
we held hands and you led me in
Swirling into memories and deja vu
Presidential sweet rendezvous
after I married you
You said I do too
Wanted to show me a whole new world
Give me a different view
Knock knock
She woke me up and told me you weren't
there, her friend said he wanted to go
back to sleep
I ran trying to get back in my dream
Stumbling to flee from the scene
I was supposed to be in bed and was
already half asleep
Back on a dark cloud scheme
Tricks from the Unseen

Not a "real" Poet

My issue with poetry is that it's made
to be read aloud
Too many meanings are in how things
sound
And not what is actually said
And too many things in poetry need
emphasis and delay
A rhythm and play on your tone
A delivery of your vibe to make the
tune
And my issue with all that is
I'm never in the mood
To seek that attention
And be validated
Snapped or applauded
My words are just how you saw them
Twist it with your own voice
So you can make your own meaning
After all my poetry is just for
reading

Diverted

Fire the foil
Straighten my spine
Each blow of smoke
Tickles my nose
Covers my eyes
A thief at night
Sneaking stealing
Peace, hope & dreams
Puffing them out
Like clouds in a stream
Of who I was
Brother and Son
Titles, labels
Divided binds
Our reflections
A false alter
My head down
A chance to score
Another breath
Just one more
Until it's the last
Promise I make
& never come back

Pick me

It's always been you
Whispers a familiar breath
At the turn of the rock
Hearts filled with anger
Disappointment
Shame

It's always been you
Tastes like a baked dandelion
Warm and sweet, with a lingering
bitterness
Weeding my heart in and out of time
Dandelion, dandelion of my life

It's always been you
Withstanding the monsoons of
heartbreak after heartbreak
As I searched for you in every garden
Pulling out the weeds to one day
reveal
The seeds you had been planting all
these years

It's always been you
After all this time magic words I
thought would whiten the heart

A remedy I hoped would be the end to a
start
Words have no weight
When it comes from an unkept heart

It's always been you
That helped carry bags of memories
through the years
Bags of tears I've cried for you
Watering the seed you planted
And just as they start to drown
You whisper

It's always been you
An admittance?
Or realization that I cannot register
You weeded me out every season of our
love
Leaving roots to dry
But today I see they haven't died

It always been you
Like a full moon reflecting the sun
Or the full moon changing the tide

12th & Jackson

Waves of us echo in the moonlight
Like dancing star seeds ready to shoot
She looked into the distance at
nothing
To find what she was looking for

The somber smoke from wood
Filled her eyes with tears

Rats dancing along the path
Their echoing squeals

Burn marks in patterns that rival the
tiles in Greece
Release the smell of tar and vinegar

Cut straws and broken pens
Bags carts trash

The thirst of bulging veins
Water cannot quench

She goes from camp to camp
Man to woman, to person to thing

Jackson where there's always action

Deals better than Black Friday

Blankets dragged across the mud
Shoes left behind

They give her the greetings
Remembering where they're from

Love stories of staying together
Tested with survival

Lights flash and the silence is
blasted
Stillness for just awhile

And on a good day you're there
With an almost recognizable smile

Not Kismet

When I asked God to distance
Me from you
I found it harder to pray
Biting my tongue so I wouldn't say
your name
The beautiful thing about you is your
name in itself is a praise
When I asked God to distance
Me from you
I stopped caring about tomorrow
Or the next day
The beautiful thing about you was
knowing you always got me
When I asked God to distance
Me from you
I couldn't let go of
All my hopes and dreams
The beautiful thing about you is
watching you succeed in everything
When I asked God to distance
Me from you
I tried to replace you with others
To rebound and bounce back
The beautiful thing about you is you
were there in the all the times he
tried to make me laugh and smile

When I asked God to distance
Me from you
I thought you'd get erased and deleted
from my memory
The beautiful thing about you is your
presence whenever I draw breath
Such is the distance God put between
us
To let you out only to gasp
At the coincidences of projections
read as signs
When I asked God to distance
Me from you
He knew he couldn't
So he distanced you from me

Lifetime Student

What I've unlearned over the years:
hiding in the back of the crowd
taking the dessert to go and eat alone
problem solving with rage
thinking I have time in the morning to
put gas
not saying I love you often
keeping in touch with people who never
text or call
trusting to easily and not trusting at
all
keeping a poker face
guilt
faith rooted in arrogance
faith rooted in innovation
childhood dreams with a picket fence
bruises are not marks of love
not all friends are companions
It's okay to wear white after Labor
Day

Part II

I said,
I got a lot of chapters that sound the
same.
He said,
So does the Quran.

Revert

I am blind yet
I still look onto the crystal blue,
with the sweet smell of dates and salt
water.
Waves crush rocks, birds flutter away.
the sun burns my skin
warms my heart
blinds my eyes.
I hear the call,
It is the first time to
humble myself.
Like the man who spoke of rivers,
I too have come from greatness
Running through my soul,
I blindly follow
What I couldn't see has become clear,
I have fallen in love
with His fear.

Fatima

I hated the idea of being a wife
I didn't know what one was or what one
did
Mama was mom
And you, Baba were dad
So when I learned you named me after
someone's wife
I didn't want to be that
Whoever she was
Then I found out there was a daughter
Who like me loves her father
And like you he loved his daughter
This made more sense to me so I said
to you and cried
"Change my name to Fatima"
I couldn't be your wife
I loved you too much
Fatima was better, she had all her
father's love
The love for his wives he had to share
I wanted you all to myself
Baba's princess
I pleaded for your years
Protesting my name
And when you took your last breath
You whispered just like him

Making me laugh and cry
That was the last time I ever wanted
to be Fatima
I've finally grown into my name
Not a wife, yet
Just a girl who had to grow up too
fast
And the keeper of your stories
When people want to know what you were
like it's me who gets to explain
That Baba was like this
And his habit was that
A legacy I hope carries on
Just like the Prophet
May peace be upon.

Third of the Night

How can I stop this mirror from
corroding?
Polish it with dust, unless you have
water
Wave patterns as I breathe you in and
out
Allah the Whole, The One
Reprise your name
He who has no son
Can I look into the mirror and not see
he who fashioned me?
He who made me seen by the unseen but
blinded me from me and the unseen?
Eyes are flawed by perception
Heart corrupted by deception
Ears whispered with the wrong message
Yet the truth lies in whatever is
reflected
Holes in my heart project your light
From tears, whispers and prayers after
midnight
And before we can witness the rising
sun
Your reflection on my mirror
Hits like an arrow gun
With more depth than the ocean

No matter how much I tarnish the
mirror
It only reflects You

Simple Sunnah Life

Allah's blessings surround you and not
even a prick can harm you
Lest He say "Be"
And even when it is
The blessing is expiation of sin

Cloud surfing because all the
companions
stopped responding
Social distances
Cut down the spread but if you can't
test
How does one determine clearance?

Religiously divert back to the many
names
Ash-Shafi, Al-Muid, Al-Jabbar
The ammunition for the Believer
Our ablution the armor that the Beloved
said to begin by washing our hands

Only those whom He wills may be guided
And from those only few know
The difference between a punishment and
test
Is that which takes you away from Him
And that which brings you close

Presents

I laid in the grass
While observing you in the clouds
Watching how the light reflects
One side
At a time

I laid in the grass
Listening to your heart in the water
Hearing each Call to return
One wave
At a time

I laid in the grass
Feeling your breath in the wind blow
across my face
Reminding me how your breath gave me
life
One breath
At a time

I laid in the grass
Fumigating in your scent that came
from earth
Basking in the floral garden beneath
me
One whiff

At a time

I laid in the grass
Parched from your beauty
Curious to your taste
One saum (fast)
At a time

Ramadan mood

She shines brighter than a Ramadan
moon
From the tears she lets out before
dawn
And the song she sings of a cave
Always in a remembrance of one His 99
names

She loves Him more than that first sip
of
Water on a hot fasting day
Almost too shy to even bring the glass
to her lips
And end the only deed that is for Him

Eyes look for him in every petal
And ripple of the sea
His voice yearned for in every
mountain top
She searches for Her beloved
While He stays lurking from the Throne

Waiting for her to call so He can
respond
Raise her hands so they may be filled

Bow down and let the weight of the
world fall
And when you rise all is at peace

I do, again

My moon star
Sparkle delight

Soaking in rays
Dancing in the beams

Shying away
Face all red

Dripped in white
Clenching your son

On your right
Giving you away

The light of love
Flows from within

Blinding those of us
Too scared to start again

Not trusting
What we can't see

But the thought of it
Is enough to know

Love is a feeling
We'll never control

Allah is the Greatest

Allahu Akbar
There is no Call
For us to stand
Feet to feet
Shoulder to shoulder
May we be guided to His plan
Allahu Akbar
Peace to Muhammad
May his sunnah we uphold
On our journey back
To our true home
Allahu Akbar
May Allah forgive
Those living and those dead
Those who were not
Even named
Yet
Allahu Akbar
Grateful and humbled although it
didn't seem fair
That at the moment I am cured from one
thing
There's a new virus in the air
And in my haste for freedom
I continued to inhale
Asalaam Alaykum waRamatullah

Inna lillahi wa inna ilayhi rajioon
YaBa'ith May you only take us when you
are pleased with us
And bring us back in honor
Before the hour
While your light still gleams
Before you awake us from this dream
Oh Resurrector, resurrect me
Resurrect us as a reflection of you

Lucid Prayers

A tear was sent to save the day
When the voice was caught and cast away
The ball of suppression lumped in my
throat
Only to be swallowed down again
Truths we never want to accept
But are never hidden from Him
Spoken aloud or left unsaid
AlSamiAlim knows us from within

Yet we carry our lies to not expose our
sins
Even after His promise is to forgive
We choke on the idea of vulnerability
Because if I allow myself to be seen
This gives you power over me
That I haven't admitted my Lord has
And if I am a true believer than I
can't give you more than Him

We know more about guilt and shame
than mercy and hope
Fear over knowledge
Refutation over introspection
Patience over dhikr
And let the tears do our bidding
A form of remembrance sweeter than
words

Words we were never taught so we never
learned

He is how we see Him
With a vow to not be left in despair
But we are
A people with no vision
A people with lost tradition
Voices lost with no heart-full of
submission
As tongues struggle to make profession
A tear dropped to save the day

Luminaries

What is a legacy
If not to be remembered?
Yet it's so much more than the recall
of a favorite moment
Or whiff of their essence in something
they used to wear
The Beloveds just call it sunnah
While the Luminaries keep it ablaze
But it's the Lovers who give it its
highest honor

Because to truly Love is to fully
submit
To what we don't know and don't
understand
To leave blank what He hasn't named
and surrender for His beautiful sake
For the hearts can only find comfort
in His pleasure

If we only shine light on the beauty
of tradition
Without loving it
We fall into the shadow of
dissimulation
Acting without preserving

Being without feeling
Turning to but never returning

While the Beloveds live and breathe
praises
In hopes of staying in a state of
remembrance
To be known as those who are often in
remembrance
All the while remembering to be
remembered only to be as soon
forgotten as our last breath

So how do we leave a legacy that is
more than just a subscription of
remembrance?
We love
Love those that taught us
Love those that showed us
Love those that hurt us
Love those that are covered in dirt
With a vow to aid their memory like
flower seeds
And not just beautiful bouquets
So that their legacy continues to grow
and bloom.

To Allah we belong, To Allah we return

I've died many times before,
What's one more?

Each stab with the dagger of
Fear to feel anything else than
Tender reminders of the suffering we
endured.

After so many deaths, one would think
I'd be aware of the signals and
patterns, but most deaths come without
a knock on the door.

The true master of seduction,
undressing wounds slowly, almost
teasing your way into feeling the
pain, but never satisfied.

Living in the moment, only to be die
the next second. Dying to be dead,
only to realize your death is another
form of life.

Praying to be in greater presence, yet
our own mirror is corrupt. Not seeing
that the answer was a reflection away.

I can't look at myself without being
terrified. After so many turns and
returns, I can only recognize the same
sad brown eyes.

Crying to go back. Laughing her way
through. Waiting in silence, for the
final call home.
I've died many times before, What's
one more?

She hoped
So she was disappointed
She prayed
And was rewarded

Self-Righteous Confliction

I pray you get Jannah
And I get in too
I pray the anger you want from me
Is an anger Allah removes from you
I pray that when you see my blessings
He gives you so much more
I pray your blessings are plentiful
So that mines you can ignore
I pray you see love in the mirror
And don't look for it in me
I pray for your peace
While I sleep blissfully
I pray in the dark
And am reminded of His light
I pray you are guided by it
And not scared to take the bite
I pray despite your hatred
To keep my heart soft
And not retaliate
I pray the rock you carry
Will soon fall off
I pray to He, who sees all

Ta'leef-to bring hearts together

The eucalyptus didn't smell as sweet
You see
The road trip over the bridge
My heart unhinged
You weren't there
And the eucalyptus didn't smell as
sweet
You see
There's been something I've been
meaning to
Say
Apologize
Share
Tell
But the eucalyptus didn't smell as
sweet
You see
To Him we belong and to Him we return
Eventually
May we meet where we were first risen
No nerves to keep us imprisoned
Besides, the eucalyptus didn't smell
as sweet
You see
There was no update on cousins Ray Ray
and Pookie

No good morning, how you doing?
Allah barely mentioned but not in your
verbatim
The eucalyptus didn't smell as sweet
You see
Our bodies as our tinder
But my belief for your cure does not
hinder
For ash-Shaffee, is the One who cures
and does not harm
But only makes pure
Because the eucalyptus didn't smell as
sweet
You see
The leaves had no scent-say to
fumigate
And the oud we burned let out a
scentless smoke
A room with new walls and no stories
to tell
So, the eucalyptus didn't smell as
sweet
You see, UC

And now I know it never will
No matter the seeds planted
It was your touch
Your quirks and smirks
Elevating lost souls of an American
ummah that lacked reflection
Who will rub the hearts like you?
There is no eucalyptus left to smell
You see
You told me what to do when this day
would come
Now it's here and I'm looking through
the notes
A guide
Because that bitter hope is gone
And my eucalyptus is back in the
ground
You see
I want to be thankful
And rejoice in the freedom of light
To know you are where you always
wanted to be
And believe that the sweet smell of
good deeds is still there
How could it not?
May Allah make it so,

Until we meet where rivers flow, and
the sweet smell of eucalyptus reaches
His throne.

Bitter grief

My eyes have become heavy
Not with bags
    Thank God.
Too many would then ask.
     Are you okay? How are things
with...
What no one wants to name.
Acknowledge the land
But don't acknowledge the truths in
each other
     Why? does my brokenness repel
you?
Have the wounds of my heart rotted and
released a stench so sweet,
Like the golden specks of pollen, you
thought would turn to honey
But was just bee shit?
    It's a thing.
Where do words of comfort from a
friend fit between guilt and grief?
The silence is clear even to the
deafest ear,
Or the inability to hold your tongue
and you keep talking over me
Like you're in a race to get to the
point

And you don't even know the direction
my emotions flow
      Read the room.
Or are we deaf, dumb and blind
Obsessed with being right
Obsessed with more wives
Obsessed with holding the line to
divide
      One God
Who has one ummah
That we both pray to in the same
language, same motions, same direction
Be, so it is.
But you tell me I don't know how to
submit
      You weren't the one sent for
mankind to follow
A lifetime of recovery from the giving
After the wool brushed on me in the
Bay
With memories of the sweet eucalyptus
of a time ago
      When I asked to examine a cane?
A time when asking was greeted with
the meeting of our eyes
That led to you serving me tea as
everyone else marveled at you

When you poured the warm rose water
over my palmed hands
And had me wipe those tired of my eyes
of mine
        That was the last time our eyes
met.

I kept praying for death
As if We know what to expect
Like grieving the living
And missing the dead

No place to prostrate

I will never know the intimacy of
companionship
I'm always an outcaste in fellowship
Too spiritual in a tradition
That requires full submission
Community imposed khalwa
Contradicting dawa
All in the name of service
Alone, but your claim is to serve us
Serve who?
Serve Hu?
Give what you love for yourself
Glorify from the heart, not books on a
shelf
We once sat knees to knees
Waiting for The Call to sip tea
Letting go of the Salafi stain
Loyal are those who sustain
Praise for the test from above
Pacing isolation with His love

Made in United States
Troutdale, OR
06/17/2024

20633192R00051